To dearest Mother
on your birthday August 14th 1975
From Neil & Nuala

OREGON HISTORICAL VIGNETTES

Sketches by PAUL KELLER
Text by JACK PEMENT

Binford & Mort

Thomas Binford, Publisher

2536 S. E. Eleventh • Portland, Oregon 97242

1974

THE HISTORICAL SUBJECTS DEPICTED

HISTORIC OREGON

As the United States has become increasingly conscious of its 200th year as a free nation in 1976, some focal attention has been directed, in Oregon, to the historic undertaking of Meriwether Lewis and William Clark by commission of President Thomas Jefferson, a founding father of the democracy.

It was their journey across the wilderness to the shores of the Pacific Ocean from St. Louis in 1805 that opened the doors of the Oregon Country for the adventuresome and hardy people of the young democracy burgeoning in the eastern part of North America.

Trappers were the first to follow in the footsteps of the trail-blazers, lured by tales of the fine-furred creatures said to abound in the Northwest. Eventually some of these voyageurs, whose link to civilization was the Hudson's Bay Company outpost on the Columbia River in what is now Vancouver, Wash., spread into the fertile Willamette Valley to try their luck at soil-tilling and stock-raising.

Experienced farmers with their wives and children came from the East, too, and if these pioneers of the Oregon Country did not prosper in terms of monetary gain, they did indeed flourish.

Oregon City, the first incorporated town west of the Mississippi, was the umbilicus of an empire. Within 43 years after it had been traversed by white men for the first time, the Oregon Country was proclaimed a territory of the United States. A sprawling possession it was, too, including vast reaches of the Northwest far beyond Oregon's present scope of 96,981 square miles.

Eleven years later—on February 14, 1859—Oregon became the 33rd state of the Union.

That progress was swift; it has remained swift. Virtually forgotten in the course of events was the incensed comment of Parson Fletcher, who accompanied Sir Francis Drake when that old pirate sailed his Golden Hind up the Northwest Coast some 400 years ago.

"Extreme gusts and flawes," the Parson protested as they neared Coos Bay, "most vile, thicke and stinking fogges."

Perhaps the old pirate should have debarked. People have been reaping the harvest of this land ever since the day Lewis and Clark set out from the other direction to find out, really, what lay beyond that veil of stinking fogges.

Farming and cattle-raising remain fundamental endeavors to this day in Oregon, but the years have brought awesome changes. Traces of Oregon's simplistic beginnings have been allowed to decay and vanish in too many instances. Only in recent years have there been people dedicated to the proposition that such artifacts merit preservation.

Paul Keller is a pioneer in this latter-day interest. He has busied himself throughout his long career as an artist in preserving with paper and ink those things he has seen changing and disappearing in Oregon. The sketches in this volume are representative of his determination to afford Oregonians a better understanding of and appreciation for their heritage.

CORBETT STABLES

Stables and carriage marquee of the elegant Victorian residence of U.S. Senator H. W. Corbett became part of a curious full block in downtown Portland for the last few years of their existence. Pressed on all sides by modern commercial enterprise, the home and its outbuildings endured for more than 60 years, finally succumbing to the crush of the central city's demands in 1936. At one time, the family cow grazed on part of the property and an eastern writer commented in bewilderment on "Portland's sixty thousand dollar cow pasture."

The residence was the scene of some of Portland's most lavish social affairs in its early years. It was built in 1875 on the block bounded by S.W. Taylor and Yamhill Streets and 5th and 6th Avenues. The stables and residence were located on a section of the property now accommodating the city's bustling bus depot. Other commercial establishments occupy the rest of the block.

OLD CHINATOWN

The once tightly knit Chinese section of Portland, although almost an entity apart from the rest of the city, lured many other citizens to its confines with twin attractions: Luscious food and honest gambling.

The Old Chinatown extended along the edge of the West Side a few blocks north and south of Burnside Street and was confined mainly to buildings that, by the time of World War II, had grown rickety and hazardous. As the old places were torn down one by one, the occupants scattered to other parts of the city, each family finding its new accommodation with no further thought of huddling as a segregated society.

The Chinese had been a part of the Portland scene as early as 1857, when Oregon's constitutional convention considered questions concerning their welfare and "regulation." The Chinese helped build the railroads of the 19th century and were resented because they were willing to work for "coolie" wages.

Only a few Oriental restaurants remain in the area today to remind Portlanders of the old "town within a town." The picturesque building portrayed here stood at S.W. 2nd Avenue and Pine Street, where now a wing of the Police Bureau sprawls.

ORIENTAL GARDENS
HOP SUEY
ORIENTAL
GARDENS
NOODLES
CHOP SUEY
PINE ST.
PAUL KELLER

THE ROBERT NEWELL HOUSE

Cherished and protected today, the home of pioneer Robert Newell at Champoeg was in a sorry state of decay when Paul Keller sketched it in the '30s. The artist was stricken by "the heavy, eerie atmosphere" of the derelict landmark close to Oregon's most celebrated historic spot.

Publication of this sketch did much to arouse interest in preserving the house. The Oregon DAR assumed responsibility for its restoration, and now it is a popular museum in an area known as "the cradle of Oregon liberty."

In his younger years Robert (Doc) Newell was a trapper, one of the West's legendary "Mountain Men." After coming to Oregon in 1842 to settle down, he prospered as a merchant and river boat operator who boasted in print in 1845 that his schedules would be strictly adhered to, "passengers or no passengers." A respected leader, he was a prominent participant in Oregon's formative government.

Newell's home, pretentious for its time and place, was located on a bluff adjoining the Willamette river town of Champoeg. It was not affected by the awesome flood of 1861 that wiped out the busy and prosperous settlement, but Newell, disenchanted, packed up and moved to the Idaho territory to spend the rest of his days.

THE ST. JOHNS BRIDGE

It was inevitable that Paul Keller's attention would be directed to the St. Johns Bridge in the course of doing his series for the Oregon Journal in the 1930s. Constructed of steel and concrete, the St. Johns Bridge is a two-tower cable suspension arch that has been described by experts as "one of the seven most beautiful in the world."

St. Johns once was a municipality separate from Portland to the south. The town was named for James John, a pioneer settler.

Ever since the bridge went into place over the Willamette River between St. Johns and N.W. St. Helens Road in 1931, people have been happily conscious of its majestic, cathedral-like attributes. It has been only in recent days, however, that the area under the structure has been improved for public use and endowed with the name Cathedral Park.

THE OREGON CITY ELEVATOR

In its long and accident-free service the old civic elevator at Oregon City traveled a distance equivalent to the moon and back. A unique undertaking as a community enterprise, the elevator was constructed in 1914 at a cost of $12,000.

The lift traveled some 28 miles a day in its 86-foot course. It carried some 5,000 passengers each 24 hours—almost as many passengers as there were people in Oregon City.

The elevator came as a boon to citizens long weary of the climb from the city's business district to the residential area above the cliff.

In 1954 the quaint wood and steel structure was replaced by a modern elevator, which is still in use. Old passengers complain now, though, that the ride lacks the enchantment of yesteryear.

FREE
OREGON CITY ELEVATOR
FISH & MEAT
REAL ESTATE
PAUL KELLER

SHOW PLACE
OF OLD SALEM

Now absorbed into the northern mall of the state capitol grounds, the area around the Cook home in Salem even in 1865 was the obvious place to locate if you wanted to see as well as be seen.

In 1855 the Legislature had moved to Corvallis 35 miles to the south in complaint against accommodations in Salem. But the lawmakers had returned to Salem in 1856 after the United States Congress appropriated money for the creation of a state capitol there. The Congress had refused to recognize Corvallis as the base of government in Oregon.

When part of the original Oregon Territory was divided to become the 33rd state in 1859, Salem was the capital city. And E. N. Cook had well demonstrated his conviction that it would endure as the capital by erecting this embellished dwelling. A wealthy man and the state treasurer, he lavished probably more than $50,000 on his residence.

The state needed Cook's land in the 1930s when the now-existing state capitol and its adjoining facilities were planned in the 1930s, and shortly after Paul Keller made this sketch the Cook home succumbed to progress. The state library was, in fact, going into position close beside the Cook home when this final glimpse of the regal, mid-Victorian Cook home was afforded.

HOTEL PORTLAND

Not so long gone that thousands of Portlanders can't remember it affectionately, the Hotel Portland was the grand old lady of Broadway for many decades. Work on it was begun in 1883 by the railroad magnate Henry Villard, but because of his impending financial distress it was not until seven years later that it was completed.

The grand opening on April 7, 1890, was a momentous occasion. "The man who comes to Portland now will find a tavern," a local newspaper commented smugly on the heels of the opening. "He needn't bring his grub and blankets."

Other than the railroads, the Hotel Portland was the first big business to provide employment opportunities for Portland's blacks. Its vital importance to them was emphasized repeatedly in editorials in the New Age, a newspaper printed by blacks in Portland at the turn of the century.

Stanford White, the noted architect who was to meet his sudden and sensational demise at the hands of Harry Thaw, was the Hotel Portland's designer. Its elegance charmed guests, among whom were U.S. presidents.

The Portland occupied the full block bounded by S.W. Broadway, 6th Avenue, and Morrison and Yamhill Streets. It was put to its ignominious death in 1951 to make way for a parking garage.

GIFT
SHOP
PAUL KELLER

THE KNIFE GRINDER

Pushing their cumbersome but fascinating little factories ahead of them, knife grinders of yesteryear seldom failed to draw a cluster of young spectators as they settled to their work on the sidewalk. They activated their honing wheels with foot pedals.

Proud craftsmen, knife grinders made their neighborhood rounds to the ring of a bell to let housewives know that their services were available. Their rules forbade intrusion into the territory of similar tradesmen, and many on their routes built up friends as well as steady customers through the years.

But alas, like the ice man, the itinerant slabwood sawyer with his smoking, keening mill affixed to his rickety truck, and "the vegetable man," the pedestrian knife grinder has walked his way into memory.

ARTHUR MATHER STORE

For 40 years ending with his death in 1920 Arthur Mather, a native of Glasgow, Scotland, operated this general store at Clackamas and served as postmaster. Once the second floor resounded to the oratory of public meetings and the happy sounds of community dances.

The store had been built before Mather came on the scene. It dated from about 1870, its lumber and windows allegedly carried around Cape Horn on a sailing vessel. When Mather spotted the place and found it for sale he hastened into the transaction, for in Western Oregon he said he had found "the garden spot of the world."

Mail was received from Portland on trains of the Oregon and California line three times a week. From this post office it was sent by rider and mail pouch to nearby settlements.

Railroad agents first knew the stop as Marshville. Other references indicate that settlers themselves called it Marshfield. When the post office was established in 1873, Noah N. Matlock, first postmaster, settled the dispute by gracing his station with the Indian word Clackamas.

A. MATHER &
DUPONT POWDER
GENERAL MERCHANDISE
BEECH NUT
BEECH NUT

THE FORESTRY BUILDING

There were Portlanders who wept openly as they watched ugly orange flames leap 100 feet above the roof of the venerated Forestry Building in 1964.

The huge log house—often referred to with pride as "the biggest log cabin in the world"—was a relic from the Lewis and Clark Exposition of 1905. Located at N.W. 28th Avenue and Upshur Street near the exposition site, it was a cavernous 206 feet long and 102 feet wide. Fifty-two matched Douglas firs, six feet in diameter, were used as its great pillars. The building was 72 feet high.

Reminiscent of a Swiss chalet, the Forestry Building was designed by Ion Lewis of the architectural firm of Whidden and Lewis, who earlier had gained respect as the designer of Cloud Cap Inn at Mt. Hood.

There was no way firemen could save the building once the unexplained flames began eating into the old logs. Five alarms were called and several firemen were injured in their endeavors to preserve the structure, but it burned to the ground.

PAUL
KELLER

COUNTRY CHURCH

Now dignified as a historic site by Tualatin Valley Heritage Inc., this long-serving church at N.W. 185th Avenue and Germantown Road no longer boasts the convenience of a carriage and horse shed, but otherwise it is going strong.

Originally called the Bethany of the Methodist Episcopal Church, it was founded by ministers from Milwaukie and Portland who went to the rural area in the Tualatin Hills to hold services in homes. It was built in 1895. Services were held in German until the 1930s. In 1960 it became an independent evangelical church and took the name Bethany Community Church.

THE KAMM BUILDING

Erected in 1884-85, the block-square Kamm Building fronting on S.W. Pine Street between Front and 1st Avenues in Portland had an elegant 200-foot facade four floors high. It was built by Jacob Kamm to house offices of the Northern Pacific Railway, which had just linked itself to Portland. The railroad meant prosperity for the city, and the Kamm Building was meant to reflect prosperity.

The main entrance included two carved figures of Atlas supporting a balcony. The interior was equally decorative.

As the years passed and more modern office space was made available in fashionable "uptown" Portland, the Kamm Building lapsed into a state of faded grandeur. Before it was demolished it was serving as nothing more than a series of dreary housekeeping rooms with one bath for each floor.

HOUSE OF HOSPITALITY

Located at what is now a bustling commercial hub at 1st and B streets in Lake Oswego, the Johnson Hotel was known as a gracious meeting place for early settlers of the area. It was constructed about 1891 by Jury Johnson.

Bereft of the porch that originally adorned its front and side, the building looked already forlorn when Paul Keller stood across the street from it, sketch pad in hand, to preserve its memory. The hotel was forced to concede the porch years before when sidewalks were laid.

For years after the Johnson Hotel ceased to function commercially two sons of the builder, Charles and James, continued to dwell on the lower floor. Present-day shoppers and business people no doubt will be surprised to learn that this location once was a place to seek comfort and quietude.

THE PITTOCK MANSION

Experiencing troubled times and looking worn beyond its years when Paul Keller visited it in 1935, the awesome residence of the wealthy but reputedly "unostentatious" (the puzzling adjective of a contemporary biographer) Henry Lewis Pittock is now restored, protected and celebrated by Portlanders as part of their common treasure.

Commanding a majestic position atop a hill on the city's West Side (known as Imperial Heights), Pittock's French Renaissance chateau affords visitors a striking portrait of the city, the Willamette and Columbia rivers, and the hills and towering, white-mantled mountains beyond. Its inner elegance attracts some 35,000 tourists each year. Public areas of the three-story, 22-room home are furnished richly and becomingly.

Pittock, who was the publisher of the Oregonian, ordered construction of his chateau in 1909. It was five years in the making. After he died in 1919 at the age of 83 his heirs found the massive residence a burden. Its maintenance was complicated and costly, its vastness grown uncordial. It was in a state of neglect when the people of Portland rallied to its cause in 1964 by raising funds for its purchase. With the added financial resources and the continuing assistance of the city's Bureau of Parks, the Pittock Mansion now is recognized as one of Portland's finest civic assets.

OREGON CAPITOL NO. 2

Loosely patterned after the national capitol in Washington, D.C., the second capitol of Oregon met the same fate of its modest predecessor of 1854—eradication by fire.

After being authorized by the State Legislature at a cost of $325,000, the second capitol began taking shape in October, 1873, when the cornerstone was laid. It boasted hollow metal girders supporting a massive copper dome, two-story porticoes faced with Corinthian columns, and mullion-windowed wings.

On April 25, 1935, the building was destroyed by a fire which rapidly spread from the basement of the east wing. Strong drafts caused in stair and elevator wells allowed the flames ready headway. Furniture, records, equipment and files were salvaged from the first floor, but most of the contents of other floors went up in smoke.

The white marble building topped by the statue of "the Golden Pioneer" that replaced capitol No. 2 in 1938 is the seat of Oregon state government today. It has been judged by experts to be one of the nation's most beautiful.

SHANTYTOWN

Sometimes called "Hooverville," the shanty-town in Sullivan Gulch was a product of the Great Depression of the '30s. For many years before that time it was a favorite place for hoboes to camp "between trains" (the Union Pacific line ran through the gulch), but with massive hard times it became an actual if flimsy village. Residents built their homes of what scrap they could cart into the gulch by foot.

Geologists say the gulch was carved into the east side of Portland as frozen deposits began thawing and moving at the end of the ice age. Its name honors Timothy Sullivan, who came from Ireland to settle on a land claim, which included the gulch, in 1851.

Fire destroyed many of the shanties in 1941, and citizen concern for safety put the final end to "Hooverville." The Banfield Freeway now cuts through the gulch.

DAYTON BLOCKHOUSE

Among the remembrances of things past that was recognized as historically important before its obliteration could occur is the Dayton Blockhouse, which really didn't belong to Dayton at all except for the fact that its citizens esteemed it and salvaged it. The structure is now a protected resource of that small Yamhill County community.

The blockhouse originally was located at the Grand Ronde Agency and was known as Fort Yamhill. It was built in 1856 and it served U.S. troops the same year. It was moved to Dayton in 1911 to become a memorial to Joel Palmer, widely respected superintendent of Indian affairs, who founded Dayton in 1849. It is honored as one of the original military fortifications of the Northwest still existent.

Baptists built the church in the background in 1886. It still serves as First Baptist Church of Dayton.

THE PIONEER WORKHORSE

Although it was known popularly as "The Pony," this little steam locomotive—the first to operate in Oregon—was a real workhorse. Manufactured in San Francisco in 1862 for the Oregon Steam Navigation Co., it replaced mules as the source of power for the four-wheel railroad cars used to transfer Columbia River freight around the Cascade Rapids. The tiny engine with the big heart averaged 200 tons of freight a day on its 4-1/2-mile track from Bonneville to the Cascades.

After only a few years of service the Pony was replaced by sturdier equipment. It was returned to San Francisco vulgarly to haul dirt. Later stored and all but proscribed, it was renovated and returned here once again for display as an artifact at the Lewis and Clark Exposition of 1905-06.

The Pony graced the yard of Portland's Union Station for many years but now is a beguiling exhibit piece at the Port of Cascade Locks. It is owned by the Oregon Historical Society.

"COUNTRY" STORE

Anachronistic in its advanced years, this venerable business house at N.W. 16th Avenue and Raleigh Street had all the burdened appearance and captivating aromas of what it once was—a country store. It had endured since 1885, and the city had merely crept out to surround it.

The suspended lanterns and brooms, the yet-functional coffee mill, the open sacks of grain with scoops at the ready, all added to the charm of the old place.

BRIDGE OVER
THE MOLALLA

Few were the covered bridges of Oregon that didn't attract Paul Keller's attention at one time or another. These members of a vanishing breed were among his favorite subjects.

This one over the Molalla River near Canby was among the earliest. It was built in the 1870s by A. S. Miller and his son, Frank, who later served as a member of the State Public Service Commission.

After some years of service as the one and only bridge in their area, citizens decided to build another. They feared that rot in the Miller Bridge timbers would cause it to collapse. It was the second bridge, however, that fell ignobly into the river one day. The first continued its faithful service for years— even for some time after notices of condemnation were tacked onto its walls.

THE KNAPP HOUSE

Nothing was too good for the glamorous wife of Richard B. Knapp, an early-day wholesale hardware merchant, and he showed his devotion by providing her with the largest, most pretentious, most costly home in 19th century Portland. It and its grounds covered an entire block between S.W. 17th and 18th Avenues, Davis and Everett streets.

Five years in the building and finished in 1882, the 18-room house was known as "the Jewel Box" for its gleaming, hand-rubbed paneled walls, its marble accessories, its elaborate chandeliers and its imported stained glass windows through which the sun sparkled rainbow rays. Less reverently, some called the place "the Owl House" for the carved birds that rested atop the ornate gables. Knapp sank the fabulous sum of $80,000 into his wife-pleasing venture.

The property changed ownership five times over the years and finally, in 1948, St. Mary's Cathedral bought the block for use as a school playground. The "Jewel Box" was laid to rest in 1951, its Victorian ghost lingering only in reverie.

AFTER THE RAIN

Towering over the rainbow, the spire of old St. Lawrence Church was a South Portland landmark for many years. In 1936 Paul Keller visited the church during the course of an early spring shower and, when the rain abated, sketched the resulting picture of majesty and inspiration. South Portland abounded with modest residences in those days, and churches and synagogues to serve the faithful were plentiful. St. Lawrence was located at 2236 S.W. 3rd Avenue in a wide area subjected to Portland's first urban renewal project in the 1960s.

AURORA SAWMILL

As bizarre an entourage as ever ventured into 19th century Oregon, the disciples of "Dr." Wilhelm Keil came across the plains on the heels of a mule-pulled, lead-lined hearse inside which was the alcohol-preserved body of a 19-year-old boy. Beside the hearse rode a German band whose musicians provided melancholy accompaniment for the singing voices of a dutifully doleful flock.

A Prussian by birth, Keil came to the United States in 1836 at the age of 24. He found himself being overwhelmed with the urge to be a religious leader in his new surroundings, and in time he was ordained a Methodist minister. When his gung-ho philosophies began clashing with those of his church elders, however, he cut his Methodist ties in a huff and formed his own cult in Missouri.

In 1855 Keil decided to move his colony to the fabled West. One who would accompany him was his son, Willie, but Willie took sick and died before the trip was begun. In bringing the boy's body to Oregon, Keil was fulfilling a deathbed promise.

Aurora was named for Keil's daughter. It was founded on March 20, 1857, along the lines of Keil's stern concept of community collectivism.

Some people have labeled Aurora a ghost town in recent years, and this rickety old sawmill that was there in the '30s would seem to foster that title, but in keeping with the spirit of its name the little community south of Oregon City is showing all the signs of a new dawning with an architectural preservation program.

THE BISHOP'S HOUSE

Tastefully restored after long neglect and coveted now as office space, this narrow Victorian Gothic edifice from 1879 originally served as the chancery office for the Catholic Archdiocese of Portland in Oregon. Once the Catholic Cathedral sat just west of its location at 223 S.W. Stark Street. Architects consider the graceful arched front a gem of 19th century design. It has recovered from an insulting life as a speakeasy, and now it is called simply but fondly "The Bishop's House."

DOWN BY THE GAS WORKS

Environmentalists would have a lot to say about it these days, but in the age before pollution was a common worry the old gas plant at Linnton, within the shadow of the St. Johns Bridge, struck more awe than protest. Its smokestack "purge," or flame exhaust, was spectacular.

The Portland Gas & Coke Co. was one of the city's first industries. In 1859 it began manufacturing gas from coal shipped from British Columbia and Australia. Its "modern" manufacturing facility was built in 1913 and endured until 1958 when it bowed to the advantages of natural gas pipelines.

YESTERYEAR
IN NEWBERG

Looking as if "High Noon" might be enacted at any moment in the dust of the street, Newberg afforded this scene of decay in the '30s. But in Newberg Gary Cooper would have been hard-pressed to find a "bad guy" to engage in a shootout, for the Quaker-dominated community was not encumbered with saloons. Although this strip of perilously leaning facades and idle wagons was called Main, it no longer was the hub of thriving Newberg. President Hoover lived in Newberg in his youth.

NEW MARKET THEATER

Located on land that had been the city's first cemetery, the imposing New Market Theater ushered in an era of cultural and social activities never before equaled in Portland. With its bold cast iron Corinthian columns, bracketed wood cornices and balustrade, and artfully executed brick work on the upper stories, the building was one of the most handsome and sumptuous in early Portland history.

The New Market Building was the concept of Alexander Ankeny, California miner and later Oregon lumber and steamboat man. Begun in 1872, the theater presented for its premiere on March 24, 1875, a production of "Rip Van Winkle" starring the acclaimed James A. Hearne. Later, Gen. and Mrs. Grant saw a performance of "Ours" at the New Market.

On the first floor of the building was a market with marble counters. The theater itself, equipped with 100 gas jets, a balcony and red plush box seats, occupied the second floor. On the third floor there was a cafe.

Ankeny died in 1891. His theater building has lived on, however impoverished its circumstances. Located at 50 S.W. 2nd Avenue, it served as a warehouse for many years and now is a parking garage.

NEW MARKET
BLOCK
1872

PUBLIC MARKET

A colorful part of downtown Portland can be remembered now by only the older settlers in this "convenience" era of supermarkets and shopping centers. In those earlier days S.W. Yamhill Street from 5th Avenue to the waterfront teemed with wagons and stalls whose proprietors, paying rent of 15 cents a day, vended fruits and vegetables, eggs, flowers, seafood and meat.

Springing up by authority granted by the city in 1910, the stalls did brisk business from the start along the curbs of the street. So popular were the little business establishments that Yamhill became useless as a thoroughfare. Not everyone was enthusiastic about that, despite the fact that the strip had acquired an important reputation as a "must" place to visit on a trip to the City of Roses.

Eventually, both to clear up Yamhill and to provide vital work opportunities in the depression, a long-planned Public Market Building was sanctioned by the city. It opened Dec. 15, 1933, amid great hopes for its future. But the enclosed market on S.W. Front Avenue never caught the public fancy like the open-air stalls had—it died in 1943. In 1947 the Oregon Journal acquired the building and converted it into a streamlined, spacious publishing house.

After the newspaper moved its operations to S.W. Broadway in 1961 the building again became derelict, the "white elephant" of old. Never again occupied, it was leveled, its site to become harborside open space.

The sketch shows lower Yamhill, with a part of the distinctive market building in the background, as it appeared in the mid-1930s.

MARKET
FRUIT
RETAIL
PAUL KELLER

WALLER HALL

Generations of students at Willamette University in Salem have held a special fondness for Waller Hall, which dates back to 1864. It is the oldest building on the campus and is admired by architects today for its classic Federal Colonial lines. It was named to honor the Rev. Alvin F. Waller, a member of Jason Lee's mission and one of the incorporators of Willamette, the oldest university in the Pacific Northwest.

SEVENTH-DAY ADVENTIST CHURCH

Despite the fact that fire had swept the West Side in 1873, destroyed all the wooden buildings in 22 blocks of the core city and left citizens apprehensive, Portland continued to grow through the use of the cheap and readily available products of the forest. Designers were adept with their Douglas fir structures, as this sketch of a church at S.W. 6th Avenue and Montgomery Street illustrates.

At first the home of a Presbyterian congregation, the church was opened for services on July 18, 1884. In 1917 Seventh-day Adventists moved in, when the Presbyterians moved out, and the Adventists finally bought the property in 1926.

The building stood until October, 1961, when Blue Cross of Oregon demolished it to make a site for its headquarters. That office building occupies the block now but is known as the Water Service Building, having been purchased from Blue Cross by the City Bureau of Water Works in the late '60s.

HAWTHORNE WATCH TOWER

Not exactly demanding work, the operation of railroad watch towers nonetheless was of fundamental importance in the days preceding ramps, overpasses, underpasses and electronic automation. With a good view up and down the tracks from his elevated quarters, the guard of this tower on the Southern Pacific right-of-way at Hawthorne Boulevard manipulated gates to stop automobiles and streetcars as trains or rail handcars approached. Between duties, the signalmen often descended from their lonely perches to laze, have a smoke and hope for the opportunity of a chat with passersby.

"DOWN THE VALLEY"

Hops are still an important crop of Western Oregon, but no longer does virtually every farmer in the Willamette Valley devote a parcel of his land to their growth. Now the tall twining vine is grown on vast acreages by farmers specializing in the cultivation of the pungent little cones important in medicine and beer-making.

Once city dwellers went into the hop fields with camping equipment to reap a farmer's harvest, to enjoy a change of routine and environment, and to earn a few dollars on the side. Now that job is done by costly machinery that a farmer can amortize only by extensive cultivation.

After the hops were gathered the small farmer shipped them to dryers like the one shown in this sketch. For many years the B. O. Shuckley dryer on the Salem-Dallas highway served the needs of growers of Polk and Marion counties.

AN OLD ORIGINAL

Surely an architect would call it a nightmare, and even its designer may have been conscious of certain shortcomings in safety, but the outdoor stairway system that once existed at S.W. 1st Avenue and Sherman Street did have a utilitarian purpose: It saved room inside the building it adjoined. Note the dismaying jumping-off point. Such jerry-built structures from early days have been all but eradicated under the city's condemnation authority.

ST. HELEN'S HALL

Although its name has been absorbed into an umbrella organization known as Oregon Episcopal Schools, St. Helen's Hall is well remembered as a privately operated seat of learning for girls. Its history is traced to 1861 when a school was opened in Milwaukie by Bishop Thomas Fielding Scott under the name Spencer Hall. It shortly became apparent, however, that Portland was outstripping Milwaukie as the hub of commerce. Within five years Spencer Hall was closed in favor of a location where the Portland City Hall now stands. That's when the school took the name St. Helen's Hall.

The 5th Avenue location proved "too noisy" with all the horse cars passing by, so in 1882 the church sold the block to the city for $100,000 (turning a profit of $90,000 on its investment).

The school next located on S.W. Vista Avenue but was destroyed by fire in 1914. Finally, in 1918, it acquired the old Portland Academy building at S.W. 13th Avenue and Hall Street. Building additions were made, but the Portland Academy structure remained the nucleus of the Episcopal school. It was this final, colorful location that Paul Keller sketched. In 1964 routing for the Stadium Freeway eradicated the school once again. In August of the same year Oregon Episcopal Schools began operations on hilltop acreage of the old Nicol estate in Raleigh Hills.

THE LUELLING HOME

Remembered as the West's first nurseryman, Henderson Luelling set out from his Iowa home in 1847 with his partner, William Meek, accompanied by wagons containing 700 young fruit trees in shallow boxes. After crossing the plains they transferred their cargo to a boat at The Dalles and from there proceeded down the Columbia and up the Willamette as far as the fertile, virgin land of what was to become Milwaukie.

Luelling prospered. It is said that in the gold rush era of California he was selling Oregon-grown apples to miners at $1 apiece.

In time Luelling built this expansive residence in Milwaukie, picturesque in its later years with its moss-weighted trees and ivy-sheltered entrance. A dedicated horticulturist, Luelling experimented in his orchards. It was he who developed the famous burgundy-colored cherry known as the Bing. This luscious summer treat was named for a Chinese servant in Luelling's employ.

PORTLAND
CITY HALL

Until this building was completed in 1895, Portland's governing body had found it necessary to sit where it could find room—usually in a new rented location following each election. Citizens were eager for their city fathers to settle down. They were tired of searching all over town to voice their complaints to and about their elected leaders.

When it was first occupied by its 34 employees, the City Hall was so commodious that it could lavishly accommodate the Oregon Historical Society's museum to taxidermal and Indian crafts. An editorial writer of the time predicted optimistically, however, "It will not be too large 10 years from now, at the rate at which the city's business is increasing." That forecast was accurate. The Lewis and Clark Exposition of 1905 brought an unprecedented surge of new business, new residents and new problems to the city.

Serving still as the heart of city government, the building has undergone so many remodelings through the years that one of its admirers from the Gay Nineties would be dumbfounded upon stepping foot into it.

Not just sentimentality has preserved City Hall. Voters have not appreciated suggestions that they dig up the money needed for a new base of civic operation.

City Hall is located on a full block bounded by S.W. 4th (the frontage shown in the sketch) and 5th avenues from Madison to Jefferson Streets. Its construction was made possible through a bond issue of $500,000 approved by the State Legislature.

SWAN ISLAND AIRPORT

Those who have grown up with the jet age surely would find it difficult to believe that once the base of commercial airline traffic in Portland was little Swan Island on the Willamette River just north of the city's hub. But it was.

Giant Ford Tri-Motors, sleek Boeing passenger ships, various private planes and non-scheduled transports used Swan Island as their base of operations for many hazard-racked years (Forest Park to the west was a deathbed) before it became apparent that this strip of north-south land was ludicrously inadequate to accommodate the air traffic that insisted on building across the continent. Varney Airlines, predecessor of United, did regular business at Swan Island.

In those early days of commercial flight, passengers were afforded chewing gum, pillows, barf bags and genuine sympathy by the brave trained nurses who had volunteered themselves as stewardesses. Chewing gum supposedly relieved discomfort of the ear brought on by changing altitudes. Above each seat, the nurses of the air dolefully pointed out to each passenger, there was a parachute available to harness on and jump ship when trouble struck. One could only chew harder at his gum in contemplation of his first leap into the void.

Perhaps even more than today, when jets swoop in and out so gracefully at Portland International Airport in routine precision, the air terminal in its bustling heyday was a Sunday mecca—a place to take the family for an interesting afternoon even though an airplane trip of one's own was beyond the realm of depression reality.

UNITED AIR LINES

YAMHILL COUNTY COURTHOUSE

At the time this sketch was published in the Oregon Journal there was a serious if splinter movement afoot in McMinnville to replace the Yamhill County Courthouse, which was built in 1888. County functions had badly outgrown the accommodation.

There were those who defended the ornate and stately structure, however, and it was not until 1962 that voters of Yamhill County finally consented to its demolition in favor of a $1 million, modern governmental center.

While the work of razing the sturdy old building was under way in 1963 its cornerstone yielded a copper box crammed with curiosities. Among them:

Prescriptions for typhoid fever. . .an obituary on the town's illustrious founder, William T. Newbry, pioneer of 1843 who was born in McMinnville, Tenn., in 1820. . .a box of pills . . .a photo copy of the Constitution. . .bylaws of Friendship Rebekah Degree Lodge No. 12. . .a petrified clam shell. . .a copy of the Boston News Letter dated April, 1704, said to be the first newspaper printed in America. . .and—most mysterious of all— some beeswax.

ALBINA

Once the hub of a town distinct from Portland, the intersection of N. Williams Avenue and Russell Street recently was relieved of a lingering distress by the Portland Development Commission in the planning of two urban renewal projects.

The landmark drugstore on the northwest corner of the intersection is, sadly, no more. However, the building's famed onion-shaped cupola of terneplate (steel coated with tin and lead) has been preserved for relocation nearby as a bus shelter or gazebo.

The two-story building with its distinctive rounded windows above the pharmacy was built in 1890 by Charles H. Hill, who was the first mayor of Albina in the days when it was still an entity apart from Portland.

Hill took pride in displaying the American flag on the building that bore his name. When the Oregon Volunteers went to the Philippines in the Spanish-American War he vowed to leave his flag in place until the regiment returned. On the day the troops came marching back "in victory and glory" he took the torn colors down and replaced them with a bright new emblem.

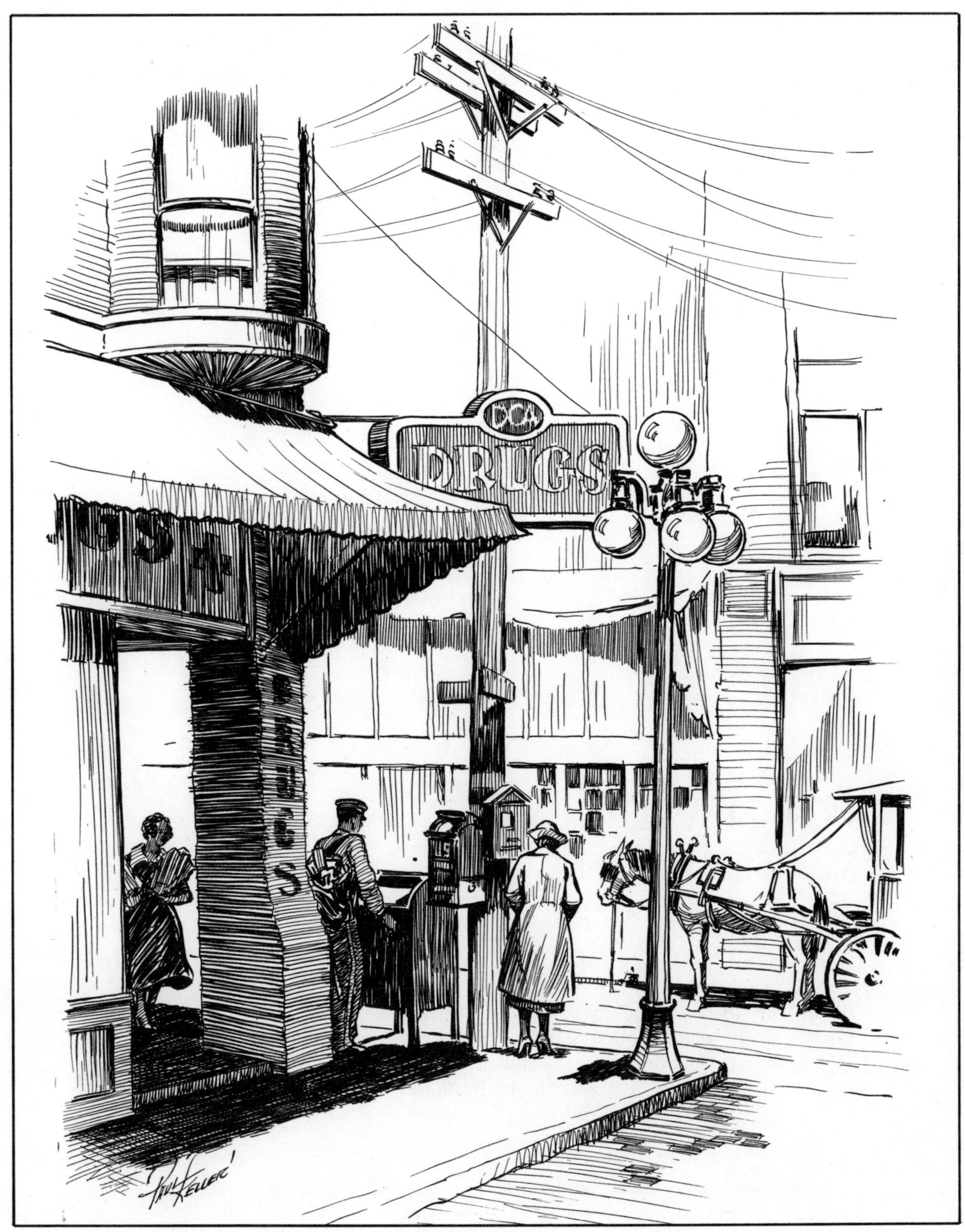
DRUGS
DRUGS

PORTLAND
WATERFRONT

The Willamette River has been of fundamental importance to Portland from the time a fragile little settlement known as "Stump Town" sprang up on its west shore. Long before the 1930s, when this scene of the old Globe dock accommodating the handsome merchantman Condor was sketched, Portland's reputation as a base of international commerce was firmly established.

The waterfront has been particularly vulnerable to tragedies. The Globe dock and elevator beside the Steel Bridge on the east bank of the river burned down in 1960 with a loss of 10,000 short tons of wheat destined for Japan. In its place went the $2 million Louis Dreyfus dock and elevator.

CONDOR

OLD MILL WHEEL

Long after its time of need this water wheel remained industrious in a secluded corner of Milwaukie at 27th and Washington Streets. When Paul Keller visited the placid scene in 1936 he found the wheel still turning belts and pulleys used to activate tools in a machine shop. It had been in constant use for over a half-century. When its "horsepower" was not needed a sluice carried the flow of water over the wheel. A setting of charm, true, but the builder had only utility in mind. Or. . .did he?

CUPOLA, DORMER AND TREE

When this sketch was published in the Oregon Journal in 1939 the Sunday editor noted wistfully in editorial comment, "Such interesting bits as this composition at the southeast corner of S.W. 2nd Avenue and Montgomery Street are becoming less and less frequently seen in Portland as the modern city extends . . ." Now, of course, such curiosities are all the rarer. Whoever was in authority when the outbuilding in the foreground was constructed, he must have been fond of trees. Notice that he accommodated one by going around its trunk in laying his roof.

OREGON CITY STREETCAR

Some of the male commuters on the huge electric cars that once plied their way between Oregon City and the downtown Portland station at S.W. 2nd Avenue and Alder Street preferred a standing position near the motorman to the wicker comfort of the passenger compartment. It was a man's world there. What idle standee didn't wonder at one time or another what cruel accident of fate had relegated him to a drab office existence rather than to the exciting and demanding life of trolley car motorman?

Swaying in its great haste, its wheels clicking a rhythmic and hypnotic song on the steel tracks, the Oregon City streetcar passed through quiet hop farms and berry fields that have yielded now to a crush of commercial and residential development. The vista afforded by trestles used to be a highlight of the trip.

The decorative head set in the wall of a building at the Portland terminal looked down on generations of commuters. But no more. . .pity, no more. . .

OREGON CITY

STEAMBOAT DAIRY

A quaint dairy operation was created at the north end of Sauvie Island after a flood inundated the lowlands. The old Mathloma, a government river boat, was towed to the island for service to the distressed cows.

The Steamboat Dairy continued to flourish for years, and eventually a barn was built adjoining the river boat. Although it endured as a dryland craft, it retained its helm and wheelhouse, a lifeboat davit and king posts. The cow in the foreground of this pastoral scene seems untroubled by any suggestion of oddity in its habitat.

THE OLD CHURCH

Forlorn and generally unloved when Paul Keller trained his artist's eye on it 40 years ago, this old edifice now has found a brand new life in its advanced years. The building at 1422 S.W. 11th Avenue in Portland originally was the home of Calvary Presbyterian Church. Its cornerstone was laid with ceremony on Sept. 11, 1882.

The church well served its original parishioners and other Christian worshipers for many years. But by the 1960s it had been libeled as an obsolescent nuisance. Then a nucleus of admirers came to the fore and rescued the relic with a public appeal for funds to restore and preserve the structure, notable for its handsome "carpenter Gothic" architecture.

The portico in the right foreground of this Keller sketch no longer exists, but the rest of the building is intact and in good repair now. Known simply as "the Old Church," it is today a nondenominational, popular place for devotions, weddings, receptions and recitals—including a weekly, unburdening "brown bag concert" during the noon hour.

BYBEE-HOWELL HOUSE

For many years this pioneer home on Sauvie Island was known as the Howell House in honor of Benjamin F. Howell, who acquired it in 1858. Now it is officially the Bybee-Howell House to acknowledge the builder and first occupant in 1856, James Bybee.

Bybee was a donation land claim settler on Sauvie Island and one of the first commissioners of Multnomah County. When Howell acquired it from Bybee the famous old house began a family ownership that was to endure for more than 100 years.

In 1961 Mrs. Rose Howell, widow of Ben Howell's grandson, was forced by ill health to sell the house. It had deteriorated to some extent and the grounds were overgrown, but its sturdy construction had protected it from ruin. Bybee had spared neither money nor effort in his home. Framing timbers were handhewn from trees on the site, and the siding was handplaned. Its six fireplaces contained brick made by the island's first settlers, and its foundation was composed of rock transported on scows from Oregon City. Doors, window frames and moldings were handcrafted of cedar. It is believed to have been Oregon's first plastered house.

Thomas Vaughan, director of the Oregon Historical Society, recognized the importance of this pioneer legacy. He led the involved campaign to acquire it for public enjoyment. The house now is the property of Multnomah County and is open to the public.

BACK PORCH
SECLUSION

Not just in the days of interstate freeways have homeowners been uprooted and inconvenienced by demands of the automobile. This once serene and shielded back porch was left exposed to the view of motorists in the '30s when the Pacific Highway was cut through the farmlands of West Portland. The house fronted on the old Capitol Highway, and the newer road left it perched desolately on the point of a triangle. The old well that motorists could now see looked inviting on a hot day.

LITTLE IRON MAN

Happily ready to accept a horse's reins on his master's behalf, this iron servant was a common sight in early-day Portland.Many homes boasted of such brightly lacquered curbside conveniences. Now they are collector's items.

Still to be seen in many curbs of Portland are the far less decorative but equally functional iron tethering rings that concrete masons routinely anchored in front of each new home in generations past. Unless the horse makes an unexpected reappearance of its own, these too will vanish with time.

TWELVE-MILE HOUSE

Much of the gimcrackery of the facade of Twelve-Mile House at S.E. Base Line (Stark Street) and Fairview Roads had been widely displayed (and perhaps even appreciated) before the late Fred T. Merrill ordered the oasis constructed in 1906. Its gingerbread, gilded lilies and little cupids had bedecked buildings at the Lewis and Clark Exposition in Portland the year before, and earlier they had been part of an attraction at the St. Louis Exposition.

In the prohibition era the oasis had a naughty if widely appreciated reputation. Revenuers closed it for awhile in 1923 and sent the proprietor to jail—much to the distress of thirsty travelers.

Also known as Plantation Inn, the gaudy Twelve-Mile House was among those landmark buildings of Oregon that met its end by fire.

Oak 12 MILE HOUSE
KELLER

THE SKIDMORE FOUNTAIN

Undoubtedly one of the most frequently photographed and drawn landmarks in Portland is the graceful (and once utilitarian) fountain bestowed on the city by Stephen G. Skidmore, a pioneer businessman. Once the hub of shopping and a rendezvous for the city's elite and tradesmen alike, the fountain is located at the confluence of S.W. 1st Avenue and Vine and Ankeny Streets.

Fashionable carriages congested the cobblestone streets in yesteryear as the city's culture-conscious made their way to and from the New Market Theater near the fountain. At night, gas lights flickered onto it. It was a place to pause, to visit and to be seen.

The Skidmore Fountain was a sort of early-day refreshment stand. Both man and beast could get a drink from it. Its trough is still an integral part of the design, but gone now are the four granite cups, fastened with chains, that used to accommodate thirsty human passersby. The cups vanished about the time Simon Benson introduced his 20 modern, "sanitary" four-bubble drinking fountains onto downtown streets in 1912-13.

The Skidmore Fountain has never lost its appeal. Nearby businesses flourishing in old buildings once facing execution by the wrecker's ruthless "headache ball" are proudly associated now in a booster organization named for the fountain.

Despite the fact that 40 years have gone by since Paul Keller began his series of Oregon vignettes for the *Oregon Journal*, the artist still hears from people hoping to acquire copies of a particular sketch they remember fondly. In all, Keller prepared 218 drawings for his weekly feature in the *Journal*. The 50 reproduced in *Oregon Historical Vignettes* have been selected for the unusual glimpses they afford into Oregon's past and, for some, their appeal as treasured memories.

Many of the structures Keller delineated so faithfully with his pen have vanished with the press of progress and the ravages of time. On the other hand, readers will recognize that a few of the fading subjects to which the artist devoted his attention in the '30s eventually were rescued and are now protected as historically significant assets.

Paul Keller, a native of Ohio, grew up in Klamath Falls and was educated at Oregon State University and art schools in Chicago. Before joining the *Oregon Journal* as a staff artist, he was employed in a similar capacity on San Francisco dailies.

In World War II, Keller served with the Office of War Information as the head of art department activities in Calcutta, India. His job was devoted to the development of propaganda directed at Burmese, Thais, Chinese and Japanese.

Now retired, Keller lives quietly with his wife in Southwest Portland. A lifelong sports enthusiast, he has occasionally prepared sport cartoons for the *Journal*. His watercolors, his favorite medium now, are in popular demand.

Like Paul Keller, Jack Pement has long been associated with depicting the Oregon scene, only his talents have been employed chiefly in feature writing rather than art. As a child he moved from Montana to Oregon, where he has since made his home. He first met Keller when he joined the news staff of the *Oregon Journal* following his discharge from the U.S. Army Signal Corps, though as an aspiring young newsman Keller's art had long impressed him.

Pement's service with the *Journal* was interrupted in 1959 for a stint as the administrative assistant to City Commissioner Mark A. (Buck) Grayson. When he first returned to the paper he was assigned to the editorial page as an associate editor, but for the past few years he has been back on the news staff, specializing in what he likes best —writing features linked with Oregon's colorful past, as he has here in *Oregon Historical Vignettes*.

104